SALTASH REMEMBERED
Part 2

Douglas C. Vosper

The Saltash Royal Regatta of 1914 beside the industrial training ship, *Mount Edgcumbe*, at her moorings. She finished by 1920; house in the trees was their sick bay. Steamer is *Prince* or *Albert* and until 1926 Mashford's boat building shed was on New Wharf, left of Clatworthy's. Saltash Garages filled in water between wharves in 1950 and Saltash cleared the land as open space in 1980.

This version of the book is virtually as originally published, presenting the work of Douglas C Vosper. There are now additional pages at the back providing information about the publisher, Arthur L Clamp.

The republishing project is being managed by Arthur's grandson, Steven Gibson. We aim to find all the research that he was involved in publishing, preserving it for the next generation as part of 'The Clamp Collection'.

INTRODUCTION

LAST YEAR I said in the introduction to A. Clamp's production of what has now turned out to be part one, that, "I hoped it would bring back interest and memories". Hearing those words often in the past year has caused this second part and I have been allowed a few more words for each picture.

Perhaps it would not be in existance but for the endless patience and help of my wife, Muriel, when pieces of paper were stuck under her nose for checking and re-reading. I can only thank in a general way those who over many years have handed me cards or photos to such an extent that I do not now know from where many came and it would not be fair to mention only recent ones. Devon Commercial Photos on page 9 is acknowledged and also British Rail on page 17.

None of these pictures appeared in the previous booklet and much building has taken place since the war. A war that made the openings that set a new building line and led to the change that has taken place on the whole of our shopping area's north side.

No doubt looking to see if Great Uncle is in a photo will give enjoyment but we must remember a lasting look at other pictures to do with "The Ancient Borough" will have a more important life here in the long run and reach a wider audience than being buried in somebody's archives. Nevertheless may the following pages give you the reader much interest.

November, 1981.

Douglas C. Vosper
Saltash, Cornwall.

Saltash Corporation Fire Brigade with their secondhand Dennis fire-engine bought in 1928 for £850 and housed in what is now "the Millbay Shop". Its largest jobs were Newton Ferrers near Callington in 1940 and Plymouth Royal Hotel and Theatre. The crew here left to right downward are Thorn, Jasper, Wall, Venn (Chief), Wells (2nd Officer), Lower, Chapman, Oliver, Southern, Garden and Dyer. Driver "Boy Deacon" is not shown.

Cover Picture

Four lines of washing, two on the beach —a right belonging to the people—was also used as a warning to some boats not to land as the police were about. On the beach by the post can be seen a duck-boat for wild fowling. Old Eli Luscombe's *Union Inn* still stands, but the "Good Shepherd Mission Hall", 1893-1945, became the Waterside Boy's Club. All other buildings shown on this side of the bridge are gone except Tamar Terrace.

Diamond Jubilee celebrations of Queen Victoria took place here 21st June, 1897. The band and "I" Company, 2nd Volunteer Battalion, D.C.L.I., marching as the 1st Devon Yeomanry ride up the other side of the street to the site of the new Victoria Gardens. Of interest is the single lamp post and pillar box standing in the middle of the street.

The 1937 Coronation procession of King George VI shows girls of County School passing Springfield Terrace with the shop of the East Cornwall Electric Supply Co. Ltd. The new position of "double lamps" were knocked down by a car in 1930 then replaced only to be finally removed by a fire engine during the war-time black-out. Smith's or Dingle's paper boy, postman Hannaford and, right of ambulanceman, T. Cockburn are in the foreground.

Empire Day (?) procession to the Recreation Ground reaches the top of Fore Street. Note popularity of children's summer hats like those then worn by sailors (Sennen hats). The gas "double lamps" post gave the name to this area, though there is still a double electric lamp standard just on the pavement; it does not stand out so the name is dying out.

Equivalent of last war's Home Guard, the 2nd Volunteer Battalion, D.C.L.I., recruited late in the 1914-18 war. Uniform was grey not khaki. Faces will be recognised from those who gave time to drill and undertake guard duty. Some names are Rawling, Gent, Porter, Lean, Howard, two Vospers, Dingle, Hosking, Henwood and a boy scout bugler. Many bugle calls were used by the services they had no radio then.

A Rememberance Day Service at the War Memorial; the cross is of a very ancient design. Some of the crowd are outside Alexandra Cottage and the entrance to Alexandra House on the corner with Albert Road. These buildings were part of the old monastic set up and were pulled down for the car park in 1963.

Led by the local Volunteer Band the August, 1899, recruiting march of 2nd Battalion, D.C.L.I., through Cornwall passing Victoria Gardens. The building under construction is 5 and 7 St. Stephens Road. We look over the site of 1 and 3 to "Jubilee Park", site of Victoria and Essa Roads leading to Laurel Bank, Port View.

Duke of Cornwall's Light Infantry (T.A.) acting as Guard of Honour for the official opening of the Tamar Road Bridge by Queen Elizabeth, the Queen Mother, on 26th April, 1962. The rate of march for the Light Infantry was 140 paces to the minute.

All the civilian population were issued with gas masks in the last war for the dreaded attack that never came. Here Capt. J. B. Nicholson, the towns chief Air Raid Warden, picks up his from the Masonic Hall, 7th June, 1939. They were carried everywhere in a cardboard box, and another piece was added at a later date.

The railway opened up Saltash from 1859 but think what the Tamar Road Bridge has done since October, 1961. Here the girder work of the western end grows out in May while another section is being constructed below. The suspension cables can be seen above the temporary catwalk.

In their crinolines thirty-six girls and teachers are seen here at Trevollard Boarding School for young ladies. Photo was taken in early 1860s when Mrs. Catherine Nepean was still head, then later a Mrs. Jasper. Built in 1709 probably by S. Wills it was empty by 1903 and has now gone.

One of the two remaining stones marking the old boundary between Saltash and St. Stephens until the 1934 amalgamation. Standing in an old orchard at South Pill it was beyond the last gas street lamp. The westernmost glass of which was painted black to stop Saltash non-rate payers receiving the light!

Using a field at Roborough in 1926 the Surrey Flying Service ran 5/- and 10/- pleasure trips and they also took photographs. One of the first in the district shows, at the top, the first Saltash Council Houses, 1924, by Salt Mill Creek, Essa Road through the centre, Lower Port View with the Friary at the bottom and allotments everywhere.

The view of the "Trot" above the bridge then filled with unwanted warships about the year 1950. The two nearest are F58 and H.M.S. *Roberts*, last of the flat bottomed Monitors. She was 8,000 tons with two 15 inch guns, a floating block buster she could get nearer to land than other ships with anything like that gun power.

Aerial an early Saltash Steamboat Co. vessel on the stocks at Commercial Wharf for an overhaul. Launched in 1865 this popular 120 ft. x 13 ft. x 7 ft. saloon paddle steamer was by 1900 used for taking "Dockyardies" to and from their work. Behind is a brigantine unloading coal at the wharf and up river are the two "Gunpowder Ships".

In 1900 this was the Post Office in muddy Forder, a building pulled down in 1955 the P.O. having moved to Apple Tree Cot, previously a tea garden. At high tides parties would even come by water to Parish Quay to view the castle ruins or visit the tea gardens; one Castle Park being in an old quarry.

Good exhaust fumes from the car in today's Old Ferry Road about 1907. Behind is Newbury's "Rustic Tea Gardens" ornamented with cork. It became Daw's Creamery, much enlarged by Cow and Gate, then Unigate; closed 1973 when thirty tanker drivers were employed. Camouflage nets also made there during the last war. To right are houses of Commercial Place which were demolished in 1941 and one man died.

Thought to have been a Pheonix Quadcar Mr. Irwin gives Mr. Trethewey a ride beside the Drill Hall around 1906. Irwin, of the bakery in North Road, behind the camera, preceded Griffin, then Seccombe when shop was demolished with others for the approach road to Tamar Road Bridge.

Saltash Y.M.C.A. football team (1919-20)—only one or two still alive—after winning the Cornwall Cup, etc. There used to be an Essa team and when they finished Saltash United took over in 1920, playing on the then sloping field, now Saltash Junior School field. Saltash Stars played where the County School was built at Cross Park in 1926.

A good example of hob-nailed boots and the last use of the town stocks at the 1938 Saltash Fair and Pageant. Formerly in store at Salt Mill depot half disappeared and the rest went after being taken to Liskeard by Caradon Council. The "prisoners" were K.B. John, G.H.R. Cook and D. Lemin.

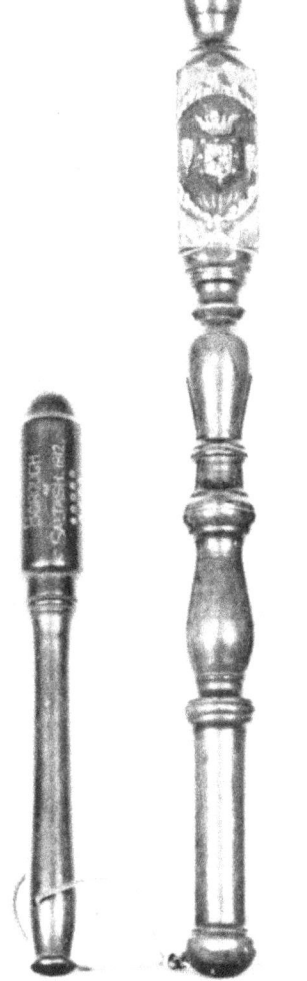

An old Saltash Borough Constables' staff and two truncheons from the Mayors Parlour photographed during the 1960s, the left hand one had disappeared by 1969! The more common type on the right is one of two. The staff has on the other side a 3 over "GR" and the date 1808.

Home of Cornwall Constabulary in Saltash on the corner of Station Road and Albert Road from 1891-1971. Barred passage window was opposite from the two cell doors. The two police houses are behind the camera, while in the shadow on the left is one of three posts to keep traffic off the narrow pavement and now removed.

The King George V Coronation procession showing firemen, band, Mayor and Corporation reaching the Wesleyan Chapel in Fore Street. Bright's fruit shop, now Gimbletts and the one behind the flag stood through the blitz and are still with us. The little houses up from the "house set back" from the building line were back-to-back cottages.

The same "house set back" is the ruin on the right of this photo after the damage of the 28/29th April, 1941, had been tidied up. The other back-to-back cottages were reached by a passage through the taller building up the street. A Mr. and Mrs. Allan died and also a Mr. Olver on the other side of the street.

On this bomb site in upper Fore Street the Regal Cinema and car park were built in 1951 then pulled down in 1964 and became the Saltash Garage showroom, 1965-73, then Pik'n Save and now AXE. Shops in 1954 picture show Cory (poultry), Fenton (off licence, etc.), Miss George (fish), London Central Meat, Scoble (fruit). On the left is Eggins (meat) and Bright (fruit).

The Old Green Dragon posting house and yard entrance was demolished for the Co-op in 1936; there is still a right of way through (103). One side of the green dragon sign, not at the moment green, is fixed to the wall below co-op flagpole Fenton the stationer and off licence and now Pengelly's is beyond.

Simon's Corner once again, do you remember some of the young people in their "Sunday-go-to-meeting-clothes" or even the railway porter maybe remembered from 1905. On the left is "The Railway Hotel" which earlier had been the *Lord Rodney* inn.

The foundation stone, now cemented over, of Albert Hall Wesleyan Mission in lower Fore Street. Laid in 1907 by Mrs. Canning Vosper (next to top hat), it replaced the use of the Ashtor Hall near the ferry landing. After its use by the Salvation Army and Methodist Youth Club it was sold and used by St. John's Ambulance (1955-72) becoming *Dwelly Hall*, named after their superintendent.

Mr. Chevers and his staff with a barge winch at the smithy at the bottom of Back Lane, now Culver Road, The last blacksmith was Mr. Bray. It was in this forge and Deacons at bottom of Elwell Lane that many on the spot jobs for the railway bridge were probably done.

Other ranks from Plymouth Division Royal Marines gave full military honours with band at the funerals of two Saltash women, a mother (1841) and daughter (1860). The former was probably unique in that a woman had a firing party. The gravestone now stands with others around St. Stephens Garden of Rememberance. They supplied the Barracks honestly with shell fish for over fifty years.

Folk gather watching efforts to drive sheep—mutton for the knackers yard—aboard the ferry in 1911. Quite a job following market at Windsor Lane or at the bottom of today's Glebe Avenue. Taken before steamboat Companies office was built on the river end of Rossiter's *Passage House* inn with its archway entrance into Tamar Street.

This painting is by Henry Martin the Saltash painter in 1898 and shows Lower Middle Street, now Albert Road. Many of these houses had smuggling hide outs and in one when pressed the whole fire-place moved; in others ladders led down. Nearest horse and cart looking into Tamar Street. 13

Opposite Cory's poultry and meat shop was the beer shop, *Tamar* inn. Beyond the window box and shutters over the lady, a man enters "gully" for steps to Silver Street. Opposite was "The Drain", on lifting the cover one tipped all the household refuse for the next tide to clear. Sun blind marks Screech's shop. Mr. Cory was one of the brothers who ran Burraton race course until 1903-4.

Boys from the *Mount Edgcumbe* industrial training ship, there were 250 of them, among the crowd at a fair on the boat beach at "Waterside" about the year 1910. Beyond the swing boats is a steam roundabout outside E. T. Bennett's *Union* inn as a "motor" train passes above on the bridge.

The remains of the old road acted as a raised footpath at Longstone until 1955. Footpath on left extended through the old hedge at the same time. To the right is entrance to Library and Junior School. "Trunk" telegraph poles and, on right in distance, "Green Tank" (water) which was removed in April, 1979.

Looking into North Road, once old Mill Lane, from Railway Hotel. Showing left to right are Saltash Radio, Seccombe (Baker), Elwell Lane, Biscombe (ironmonger), Co-op (garages), Joan (hairdresser) all pulled down in 1960 for the bridge roundabout. Still standing are parts of Visick's (watchmaker), Thornly (draper) and, not seen, Vosper (bootmaker); on the left were Howarth (barber) and Gimblett (fruiterer).

The eastern entrance pillars to Port View Private Estate, removed in 1930s; other end were balks of timber with a chain between. Once a year the chain was removed and placed between these stone pillars to emphasise "private". Large trees were planted by boundary wall pavement, first one was removed in 1963. Higher Port View numbered 1964 and carried on to St. Stephens Road.

Unveiling in the Victoria Garden on the 18th September, 1901, of the memorial in two types of granite to Major-General Sir William Penn Symons, K.C.B., of Hatt by Lord Mount Edgcumbe. He was the first General killed in the Boer War, dying at Talani Hill (official spelling) in Natal, 20th October, 1899.

After sixty years reign the Victoria Gardens opened 21st June, 1897, marking this period. The dedication in the photograph, then the tennis court portion, while in the then Longstone Road stand the 1st Devon Yeomanry. Mary Littleton of "Well Park" conveyed the land on 24th June, 1897, to the Council, *not to be built on to the detriment of the properties.*

Our Queen as Princess Elizabeth visited East Cornwall on 21st October, 1949. Here she inspects cubs and brownies before boarding the ferry. Adults are *Brown Owl*, B. Crabb, *Scout District Commisssioner*, D.C. Vosper, B.E.M., and *Duchy Land Steward*, T.M. Stanier. Many people must remember *Lady Cubmaster*, W. Gard, and the town dramatic shows she produced in the church rooms.

Brunel's world famous Royal Albert Bridge takes shape between Saltash Passage and Saltash in 1857. Probably this is a Sunday as not a workman is in sight. Photos of this date show St. Nicholas Church tower with its four sided short spire. Other buildings are *Passage House* inn, Ashtor Hall and Rose Cliff.

Signal box and steam locomotive filling arrangements at Wearde, once Defiance Halt. Used as a carriage siding going away to the left is the track of the old Cornwall Railway. Passing under the lane's hump backed bridge removed 12th January, 1873, is still a right of way to Point Field. Above the tank is seen the present double track opened in 1908.

May, 1908, the G.W.R. opened a new section inland to avoid costs caused by existing crossings of tidal creeks. In front of the new Forder viaduct is the old Cornwall Railway timber structure from Point Field to Antony Passage being taken down. The size of the timbers can be judged when compared with the adult to right.

Last day of the regular local steam "motor" train service on the 12th June, 1961. One on the loop line lets off steam while a coach and wagon are at the goods shed; two milk floats are to the right. Goods yard closed save for milk July, 1962, then taken over by the flower growers and all closed when the station became unmanned on 11th December, 1971. All the fields shown are now built over.

A 6400 class pannier tank locomotive fitted for auto-train working receives water from tank at railway station between 1914 and 1968 Before the road bridge was opened there were 52 local trains a day and coaches seated 80 plus standing at peak periods.

Eighty-six feet high, Brunel's 201 yard timber viaduct of the Cornwall Railway across Coombe Creek at Saltash (1859-94). New stone for the double track can be seen behind where two steam cranes are working. This used to have a footpath on the west side for sailors to walk between Wearde Quay and Saltash station for H.M.S. *Defiance*.

Prior to 1903 what a different St. Stephens village! The *Church House* inn was then replaced by the *Cecil Arms*. In the wall behind was a stone coffin lid, now inside the Church (1278). In the plot by the road two stones list boys from the *Mount Edgcumbe*, "—buried near at hand". Up the farm lane is the murderer's plot and in the right foreground is thatch of a mangle or turnip clamp.

Used from 1891 to the blitz of 1941, Wesley Centenary Memorial Chapel stood on the site of today's Post Office having moved from below the Guildhall. Had reopened in January, 1911, after making changes including the window and facing with surplus stone from the G.W.R. bridges on their new length of line (1908).

Gas jet lighting, walls plastered (1868-1930), stone pulpit and reredos removed. From about 1270 it closed for 160 years by major excommunication for some reason; St. Nicholas became a parish church in 1881. On land claimed by the ancient Saltash Corporation it was unique in ecclesiastical history, even the bell rope was bought from the rates until 1924 and the "chaplain" had to obtain the key from the Mayor to enter!

18

Presentation of long service medals to firemen at a dance in 1924; the Brigade was formed in 1898. Town electricity started in 1924 so here the Guildhall had both gas/electric fittings as gales would often put the latter out. Unfortunately the reflection of the light has stopped the Charles II Royal Arms of 1661 showing in the frame above the word "Welcome". It disappeared about 1944.

Longlands Board School built for 160 children was opened in January, 1876, and closed in 1958. At one time boys over six years from St. Stephen's school had to walk to Longlands for school. First master and mistress from St. Stephens was John Oats and Miss Barron of Trematon.

Bennett and Palmer's three ton Foden steam wagon used from 1915 to 1930. Driver Harold Marks and assistant, Nelson Olver, have unloaded stone for building the County School during 1925-6. Started from cold each day the water tank lasted for 20 miles. Only other steam vehicle was a five ton Mann iron-tyred lorry belonging to Jefford's of Torr Quarry.

An engraving by E. Finden from a drawing by W. Westall, A.R.A., who was here about 1829. This early bridge where tidal movement ends was pulled down in 1876, the road passing right behind *Sportsmans* inn. Now the *Notter Bridge* inn, nestling below the overgrown Notter Tor or Hole's Rock on the Lynher, river of old quarries.

Shortage of change in some centuries caused traders to produce tokens. This two centimetre brass one reads around a sailing ship—perhaps a river barge—"1667. Peter Stephens of", the other side "Saltash in Cornwell" around "His half peny". Charles II killed them by issuing large numbers of ¼d. and ½d. from 1670.

Below South Pill at the top end of Bennett's Marsh stood St. Stephens Sewage Works (St. Germans R.D.C.). Built in 1881 for pipes laid in parts of the parish, this obsolete fill and draw method was built on high walls due to land gradient. It came to an end in 1975 when linked to new treatment works at Coombe.

In two halves, the greenish black wax 1683 Borough Charter seal of Charles II. It is about 6" across and the other half shows him on horse and includes the lily of France and the Royal Arms. Mystery! There were two seals both cut in half as a pair which were disposed of in a sale after the war and now in private hands.

A heavy weight with the arms of Saltash sunk into it (a boss, the die of which is missing) used for pressing the design on metal or buttons on the Town Sergeant's uniform, etc.

The plaque over the north door of S.S. Nicholas and Faith Church. It reads: "THIS CHAPPLE WAS RE-PAIRED / IN THE MAIRALTY OF MATHEW / VEALE GENT ANNO 1689". This shows it was the Corporation Chapel and that its repair was not an ecclesiastical matter.

Abdhu Cotts, at the junction of Fairmead and Liskeard Roads; with communal toilet and wash water at the back through archway to left of which was the pump—morning was the time to see the bucket procession! These little places were demolished in 1964-5 and were fitted with "coffin drops", part of bedroom floor that lifted at times of death and no doubt furniture moving.

There was in 1883 *The Ploughboy*, then a Bound House. The two slate-fronted cottages were included and heightened at a later date. King's Cottages to right and all those behind the girls were removed for the new layout of the A38 road in 1962. Note old Salt Mill sewer works vent pipe.

Buller arms and plaque on the two little almshouses cottages erected to the memory of James Buller of Shillingham in 1726. The family was important in St. Stephens parish for centuries and even have a shelter (?) among their grave stones in St. Stephen's churchyard.

Loading shutes at Quarry Quay Forder, the stone was brought by cart, steam wagon and then motorised tramway in the 1920s. Until the road came this was the route toward Antony Passage—mill lake seen under viaduct—there was a 4-5ft. post which, if covered by water, indicated that it was dangerous to proceed around even for a horse.

Remains of old tidal mill building at Antony Passage showing the out flow openings to take the used water of the tidal pond away from the three water wheels used to rotate the four grinding stones. This building dates from 1613 but the mill pond dam is 1400 odd.

These were the green fields from Burraton Coombe to St. Stephens Church; Church Town Vale at top left, bottom is the old tannery of 1842 with ventilation louvres closed. S. C. Adams started his business beside the Latch-Brook around 1834. Where the road goes left around field it was later diverted into Bryansway and the top filled in in 1973.

Inland from Ince Point, River Lynher, is Ince Castle, shown in 1904, walls plastered and with four turrets. Said to be built 1540, it is rare in Cornwall being built of brick. Garrisoned for the King in 1646 it was left in isolation to surrender. Much done to restore it from a farm during the 1930s and rebuilt inside in 1961.

Ordnance Survey map of 1889 showing the Saltash of that time and its boundary. High Port View is called *Sumack Road*, one wonders whose homes now stand on Lollaberry Quarry while the house of Cross Park is in the St. Stephens-by-Saltash countryside.

Rare today a cattle pound across the road from Manor Farm, Trematon. Unfortunately the 8-10 ft. walls were reduced in the 1960s to a height of the entrance lock stone. Now marked by Caradon plaque, stray animals were impounded until the owner came forward and paid legal charges. There was once one at Higher Burraton.

Arthur L. Clamp – the man behind the books

Arthur Leslie Clamp was a man of boundless energy with a passion for helping others, particularly through his love of history. A printer by trade, he started his career in a printing company before moving his family from Exeter to Plymouth to teach at the Plymouth College of Art and Design, where he eventually became the Head of the Printing Department.

A Devoted Family Man

Despite his love of teaching, Arthur prioritised his family, always making it home by 5:30pm for tea. He and his wife, Rosemary, raised five children: Susan, Angela, Elizabeth, David, and Steven. Arthur would often combine his love of family and history by taking his children on Sunday walks, encouraging them to appreciate historical monuments by taking photos or making crayon rubbings of gravestones for his books. The family home at 203 Elburton Road was a hub of activity, with a large garden, featuring a two-storey fort and a makeshift swimming pool.

Arthur with his five children.

A Lifelong Learner and Adventurer

Arthur's thirst for knowledge extended beyond history to a deep curiosity about the world. He was passionate about exploring different cultures, traditions, and cuisines, often taking advantage of his long summer holidays as a teacher to travel to places like India, Russia, South America, the middle east and the USA, sometimes bringing one of his children along. This adventurous spirit even influenced his home life, as seen by the short-lived family tradition of steam-cooking vegetables after a trip to Iceland.

History is a prominent feature of family days out

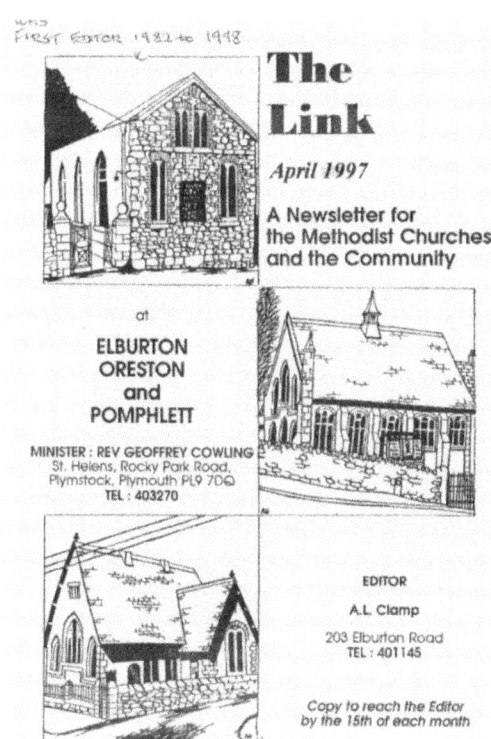

Community and Philanthropic Spirit

His commitment to serving others was evident in his long-standing involvement with the Elburton Methodist Church. He was the Sunday School Superintendent for over 15 years and served as the editor of the wider church's monthly newsletter, "The Link," for a similar duration. After Rosemary's very sad passing, Arthur later remarried and, following a chance encounter with a professor from India, established a connection with a missionary school in Chennai. Together with his new wife, Christine, he co-founded a "Sponsor a Child's Education" program that continues to this day.

*Pictured left – The cover of 'The Link' complete
with hand drawn sketches of each church by Angela
Below right – Arthur Clamp promoting his latest book
Below left – Arthur at home with his first wife, Rosemary
Below centre – Arthur on holiday with his second wife,
Christine*

A Legacy of Learning and Positivity

Arthur's greatest passion was history, which he brought to life through tireless research, documentation, and the many books he authored. He was driven by a need to "never be stuck in a rut," constantly seeking new experiences, meeting new people, and expanding his knowledge. With a positive attitude and a great sense of humour, he was always ready to help others, leaving a lasting impact on his family and community. His children, Susan, Angela, Elizabeth, David, and Steven, remember him with love and gratitude.

David Clamp, 2025

A Legacy of Local History

Below is the story of how Arthur L Clamp began writing books, in his own words, drafted shortly before he passed away in 2001. I have only made minor alterations to this text, correcting grammatical errors that he did not survive to correct himself. When I first discovered this text, I was shocked to see my name mentioned. It seems that, unbeknownst to me, I shared my first PC with him. I suspect he used it during the day when I was at school, although I do have one memory of sitting with him and showing him how it worked. It has been a pleasure to pick up where he left off and see his books republished and redistributed, and to know that I was part of the story, even back then. It was also fascinating to discover that his pricing structure matches the way I have tried to price the books, with a third going to local sellers and the rest covering printing costs with a little left over for my expenses.

I am his eldest grandson, and it is a privilege to curate his legacy, which we are calling 'The Clamp Collection'. The very last line of the text originally reads "The following pages list all the titles." Sadly, that page is missing and we have no record of all the books he published and knowing that some of those were researched by other authors makes the process of finding them even harder. I look forward to one day completing the collection and seeing them all available again. And maybe, one day, I'll even start writing my own to add to the series. For now, here is his story in his own words.

Steven Gibson, 2025

Writing and Publishing Booklets on Local Topics and Areas

I started this interest in either 1968 or 1969 when living in Woodford. I had by these dates established the Department of Printing and I think I must have been looking for something different to do. The first titles were of A5 size proofed from type set at Clarke, Doble and Brendon, Ltd., Plymouth printers, and then made up into pages and printed at Sawtell and Neilson, Ltd., Totnes.

Then began a slow process of getting them out to shops, etc. which proved to be more time consuming and difficult than actually researching, writing and getting the books into print. However, I persisted and opened a business account with Barclays Bank on the Broadway. I was advised to give it a title so I called it "Westway Publications". There came along another problem, one of storage of paper and finished books which was solved when the family moved to Elburton in 1970.

I changed the printer to Penwell, Ltd., Callington, Cornwall, as he was then just setting up himself and his prices seemed very reasonable. I did not get any of the printers to make up the complete books. I hand folded the flat printed sheets, stitched the books on a small manual table stitcher and trimmed them in a small hand turned guillotine which I bought from someone in Penzance for £40. It was brought up in a van.

The trouble and time going to and fro to Callington was too much so I transferred the printing to PDS Printers, Prince Rock, Plymouth, and I have been with them ever since. Now they are at Plympton which is easy to reach and they fold the flat sheets which was turning out to be a long chore which only saved a small part of the printing costs.

All my first titles were written by myself. I took the photographs and developed them in the loft of the house, the type was set by now on a computer situated in the house at Elburton from which I had collected photographic lengths of text to cut up and law down as pages.

At some point I decided that I would do my own film processing of lith film so I bought a large second hand process camera from Kingsbridge and learnt through trial and error to make line negatives of the text and halftone negatives of the illustrations which proved more difficult than I anticipated. The main problem was trying to keep the developer in the large dish at the correct temperature as any change would affect the developing time. I replaced this old camera with a brand new one bought from Croydon, Surrey, costing £900. This has turned out to be a great asset cutting out an expensive part of the printer's costs and one crucial aspect of the work which I could control.

By the middle 1970s there were many outlets I had contacted in Plymouth, up to Dartmoor, Exeter, around to Torbay, Totnes, Dartmouth and the South Hams. The market for local books was much greater than I had first thought and through getting to know many local people undertaking research themselves had the chance to help and make up books for other people who had in most instances, got together a collection of photographs with some text in a rather muddled way. Through my experience in print I was able to shape up their work and get it into print and in every case I had to pay the printer and let the person have the royalties. In the majority of titles produced in this manner this was another way of producing titles and it did give some profit to my work. However, I must say that in a few cases I lost out by either the other person getting the numbers wrong, not returning any monies from stock I delivered or they thought that more of their books should have been sold.

The print run was usually 1,000 copies and from time to time I have had reprints of 250 copies. It took about ten years to clear the first print run so I always had large stocks in the garage, workshop, etc. The numbers sold during the early years was about 7,000 copies a year increasing to around 9,000 copies and for the whole of the enterprise about 500,000 have been sold. The booklets have become part of the local scene and many people collect them, shops regularly order copies and I go around certain areas month by month restocking or replacing titles as necessary.

During the past year or so I have started setting the text on a Packard Bell PC, something which I should have done some years back. I share it with Steven Gibson, my grandson. There appears to be no end to the market for local books, but I could not earn a regular income because of the long time it takes to sell stock.

However, now exceeding 100 titles made up mainly of A4 twenty-four page booklets, some folded guides, with selling prices set with a third going to the shop which is the trade custom, the original idea has been quite successful and could go on for ever.

Apart from monetary benefits, however spasmodically these might be, I have learnt a lot myself, met many interesting people and have become part of the local scene with requests to give talks and to advise people about getting into print.

Arthur L Clamp, 2001

This newspaper article, published by the Evening Herald on 17th August 2001, forms a good record of his life. Just as he encourages us to learn more about local history, we encourage you to learn a little about him. For that reason, we have included these pages at the back of all the most recently republished books, in honour of his memory and recognition of his contribution to the community.

www.ingramcontent.com/pod-product-compliance
Lightning Source LLC
Chambersburg PA
CBHW061408070526
44584CB00031B/4189